The Other Night Before Christmas

ISBN 979-8-88943-846-5 (paperback)
ISBN 979-8-88943-847-2 (digital)

Registration Number TXu 2-355-444

Christian Faith Publishing
832 Park Avenue
Meadville, PA 16335
www.christianfaithpublishing.com

Printed in the United States of America

The Other Night Before Christmas

Candice Schultz

'Twas the night before Christmas long ago and far away
in the land of Judea, so the holy prophets say.

Some shepherds were watching their flocks in a field,
and the little town of Bethlehem slumbered just in view.

The night was crisp and really rather cold, so the
    shepherds huddled together, and told stories of old.

The heavens above were ablaze with bright stars,
especially one large one that seemed to come from afar.

"Doesn't that star seem awfully large?" asked one shepherd to another, as he pointed to a large star in the East.
"Yes!" responded the other shepherd. "Compared to the ones I've seen, that is like no other!"

As they were talking, a loud, whirring, rushing sound filled
    their ears, and the shepherds gasped as they saw an angel
    ever so near!
The shepherds were quaking and terrified at best to think
    something like this could disrupt their rest!
And that was not all, for the angel who joined them was from God,
    as the radiance of the LORD's glory surrounded them all.

"Don't be afraid!" exclaimed the angel. "I come to proclaim
    the good news that will bring you great joy that will be for
    all people!
For the Savior, who is Messiah the LORD, was born today.
    He lies in a manger in Bethlehem, the City of David.
Now go and see, and you will come back in a new form of
    humanity!"

Suddenly that angel was joined by many angels known as the Armies of
  Heaven.
They were singing and praising God and shouting:
    "Glory to God in the highest heaven!
    And peace on earth to people He favors!"

Then the angels were gone, and one shepherd could hardly speak except
    to whisper,
        "Let's go and see, even if we do feel somewhat weak!"
"How can we leave our sheep?" nervously asked one shepherd to another.
        "They will be in such a fright!"
"Don't worry," replied the other shepherd. "The LORD will be their
        Shepherd on this Holy Night!"

So across the pastures they trod, with a couple of lambs as gifts
        shielded next to their breasts.
The huge star moved as it showed them the way
        to a hovel in Bethlehem, where animals eat their hay.

There, a light so bright shone out of the door that the shepherds,
    though unsure, could only slowly draw near.
They crept closer and closer, their lambs in their arms,
    and looked inside.

And there, much to their alarm, lay the Child—Perfection at Rest—
    warmly swaddled in a heavenly nest!
For though the Babe was lying in a manger so rough,
    He was being bathed in holy, heavenly light from above,
as the mother and father looked on in love.

The shepherds asked if they could come in and present their
    gifts to the Messiah the LORD.
And the mother named Mary said, "Of course! His name is **Jesus**.
    He is the **Son of God** and **Savior** of the world.
He will take away our sins—from you and from me—
    so someday we all in heaven will be!"
Then the shepherds laid their lambs down as gifts for the Babe.
After being blessed, they went on their way.

"What a night!" one shepherd exclaimed, as they made their
    way back to the field.
"What started out so quiet became life-changing at best,
    for now we are going to heaven!
Oh, how we are blessed!"

A Special Prayer

Would you like to someday go to heaven like the shepherds? Then please pray this prayer out loud:

Dear God, I realize that I have sinned against You and that I cannot save myself. I desire to turn from my sins and follow You. I believe that Jesus Christ died on the cross and shed His blood to cleanse me of my sins. I believe He rose from the dead so that I might have eternal life. I ask You, Jesus, to forgive my sins and come into my life. I pray this sincerely. Jesus is Lord!